Brown Mouse gets some corn

Story by Jenny Giles
Illustrations by Pat DeWitt-Grush

2

Brown Mouse looked out the window.

"I can see some corn
in the garden," he said.

"I like eating corn," said White Mouse.

"Let's go and get some!"
said Gray Mouse.

4

"But we can't," said White Mouse.

"The cat is outside.

He will get us."

"Look!" said Brown Mouse.

"The dog is asleep

down here by the window.

We can wake him up,

and then he will run

after the cat.

Let's go!"

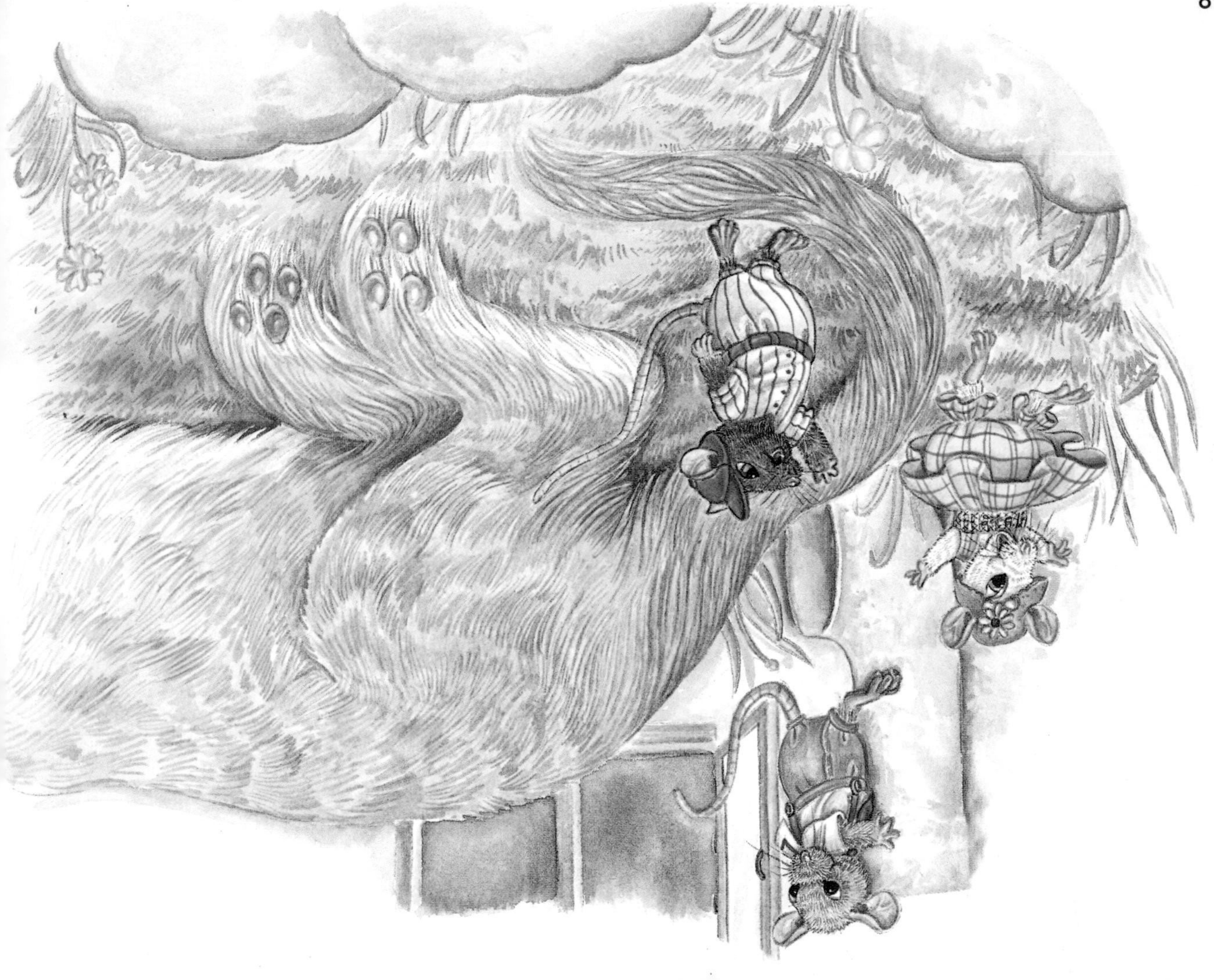

The little mice
climbed out of the window.

"Come on," said Brown Mouse.
"Let's all jump on the dog's tail!"

The little mice
jumped up and down
on the dog's tail.

The dog woke up.

Then the dog saw the cat.

"Grrr!" he said,
and the cat ran away.

The dog ran after it.

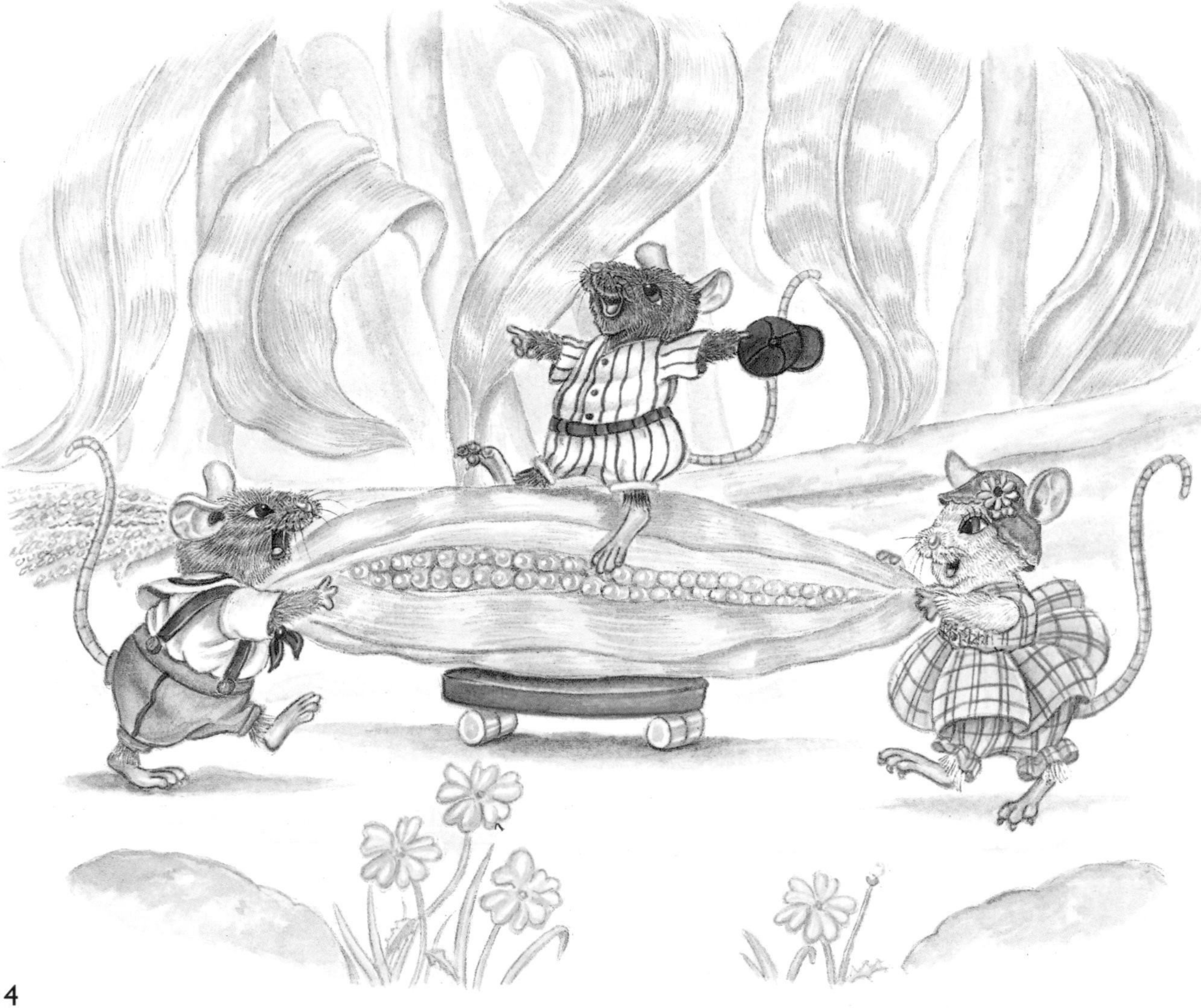

"Now we can go and get the corn!"
said Brown Mouse.

The mice ran to the garden
and came back with some corn.

"We love eating corn,"

said the three little mice.